# DISCOVERING

◆

# IRELAND

## By Philip Steele

*A ZOË BOOK*

## A ZOË BOOK

© 1996 Zoë Books Limited

Devised and produced by
Zoë Books Limited
15 Worthy Lane
Winchester
Hampshire SO23 7AB
England

First published in Great Britain in 1996 by
Zoë Books Limited
15 Worthy Lane
Winchester
Hampshire SO23 7AB

A record of the CIP data is available from the British Library.

ISBN 1 874488 63 0

Printed in Italy by Grafedit SpA
Design: Jan Sterling, Sterling Associates
Picture research: Bob Davidson
Map: Gecko Limited
Production: Grahame Griffiths

## Acknowledgment

The author and publisher wish to thank Roibeard Ó Maolalaigh, Director of *Ionad na Gaeilge*, Centre for Irish Studies, at the Department of Celtic, The University of Edinburgh, for advice and assistance with this book.

## Photographic acknowledgments
The publishers wish to acknowledge, with thanks, the following photographic sources:

Cover: Zefa; title page: Impact/Geray Sweeney; 5l Impact/Michael Dent; 5r Zefa; 6 Impact/Michael George; 7l Robert Harding Picture Library/ Dominic Harcourt-Webster; 7r Impact/Brian Harris; 8 Robert Harding Picture Library/Roy Rainford; 9l Impact/Paul O'Driscoll; 9r Impact/ Bob Hobby; 10, 11l Robert Harding Picture Library/Philip Craven; 11r Allsport/Mike Hewitt; 12 Impact/Bruce Stephens; 13l Robert Harding Picture Library/Duncan Maxwell; 13r Impact/ Michael Dent; 14,15l&r,16 Impact/Geray Sweeney; 17l Impact/Michael Dent; 17r Impact/ Geray Sweeney; 18 Robert Harding Picture Library/Roger Stowell; 19l Impact/David Reed; 19r Impact/Geray Sweeney; 20 Impact/Paul O'Driscoll; 21l&r Sporting Pictures (UK); 22 Robert Harding Picture Library/Dominic Harcourt-Webster; 23l *William Butler Yeats* by Augustus John (1878-1961) Manchester City Art Galleries/Bridgeman Art Library; 23r, 24, 25l&r Ancient Art & Architecture Collection; 26 Philip Sauvain Picture Collection; 27l Mary Evans Picture Library; 27r Philip Sauvain Picture Collection; 28 The Mansell Collection; 29l Impact/John Arthur; 29r Impact/Geray Sweeney

The publishers have made every effort to trace the copyright holders, but if they have inadvertently overlooked any, they will be pleased to make the necessary arrangement at the first opportunity.

**Cover:** *Blarney Castle, County Cork*

**Title page:** *The Giant's Causeway, County Antrim*

# Contents

# Northern Ireland

Area: 14 120 sq km
    (5 452 sq miles)
Population: 1 610 000
Capital: Belfast

# Republic of Ireland

Area: 70 285 sq km
    (27 137 sq miles)
Population: 3 512 000
Capital: Dublin

Malin Head

SCOTLAND

Coleraine
L Foyle
Londonderry
R Foyle
Antrim Mts
North Channel

Donegal

NORTHERN
IRELAND
ULSTER
L Neagh
Antrim
Belfast L
Belfast
Strangford L

Donegal Bay

Lower L Erne

Killala
Bay
Sligo
Enniskillen
Armagh
Downpatrick

Upper L Erne
Mts of
Mourne

Isle of
Man

Cavan
Carrickmacross
Dunkalk
Dundalk Bay

R Shannon

Achill Island
Clew Bay
Castlebar

Irish Sea

Roscommon
Royal Canal
R Boyne
Drogheda

CONNACHT
L Ree
Athlone

Galway
REPUBLIC OF
IRELAND (Éire)
Grand Canal
R Liffey
Dublin
Dún Laoghaire
Bray

Galway Bay
Kildare
Wicklow Mts
Glendalough

Aran Islands
Lisdoonvarna
L Derg
LEINSTER
Wicklow

Atlantic Ocean

Silieve Bloom

Kilkenny
R Slaney

Limerick

Tipperary

Tralee
MUNSTER
Wexford
Rosslare

Dingle Bay
Killarney
Waterford

Carrantuohill
(1041 m)
R Lee
Cork

St George's Channel

WALES

Bantry Bay

N

0          80 km
0       40 miles

# *Céad Míle Fáilte!*

'One hundred thousand welcomes'! Ireland (*Éire* in the Irish language) lies on the northwestern edge of Europe, facing the stormy waters of the Atlantic Ocean. It is the second largest island of the British Isles, and is separated from the largest (Great Britain) by the Irish Sea.

Central Ireland forms a broad rolling plain. It is a region of peaceful farmland, peat bogs and river valleys. This is ringed by ranges of hills and low mountains. The Atlantic breakers have worn away a ragged coastline to the west, with sheer cliffs, inlets, bays and offshore islands. Warm ocean currents bring a mild, moist climate to Ireland. The country's green fields have given it the nickname of 'the emerald isle'.

*A small post office in the Republic of Ireland*

*A traditional farmhouse in the countryside*

## A divided island

Ireland is divided into four ancient parts, or provinces. They are Connacht, Munster, Leinster and Ulster. Since 1605 the provinces have been sub-divided into 32 counties.

Six of Ulster's nine counties make up Northern Ireland. Together, they are governed as a province of the United Kingdom. The other counties make up an independent country, the Republic of Ireland.

### Questions of language

English is spoken throughout Ireland, but on street signs, banknotes and buses you will see words in Irish Gaelic. This is a Celtic language, which is closely related to Scots Gaelic. Irish is taught in schools in the Republic and by some groups in Northern Ireland. More than 30 per cent of people in the Republic understand Irish. The country areas where Irish is widely spoken are called *Gaeltachtaí*.

# The far west

The province of Connacht (*Cúige Chonnacht*) includes some of the most beautiful scenery in western Europe. Blue hills rise from dark peat bogs, and donkeys graze in peaceful green fields. There are shining lakes and broad rivers full of salmon and trout. Cliffs, noisy with gulls, stand high above the Atlantic waves. Long, sandy beaches are pounded by surf. In summer there are fields of wild flowers and hedges of crimson fuchsia.

Parts of this landscape are very bleak. Farming is hard in some areas, and much of the region is poor. The loneliness and peace enjoyed by visitors is really the result of a tragedy. During the past 150 years, many people have had to move away. They travelled to Dublin, England, Australia and the United States in search of work and a better life.

## Layers of turf

Peat bogs are made up of matted, waterlogged plants. Over the past 8000 years, layers of rich black peat have formed, 6-10 metres thick. Dried peat burns well as fuel. People use long spades to cut it. They stack it in piles outside their farms and cottages for the winter.

Bogs are the home of insects and wetland birds. Wild flowers grow there, such as tormentil, sundew, bog bean and bog pimpernel.

## To the holy mountain

Galway (*Gaillimh*) is the southernmost county of Connacht. Galway City is the chief town on Ireland's west coast.

*The west coast and the Atlantic Ocean*

Currach *rowers in a race*

Lough Corrib lies to the north, and beyond it, Galway Bay opens out into the Atlantic Ocean. The Aran islanders still fish from open boats of tarred canvas, called *currachs*. Connemara, with its national park, is one of the most beautiful regions of Ireland. It is famed for its ponies.

The coastline continues northwards to County Mayo (*Maigh Eo*). It takes in the scattered isles of Clew Bay and the looming peak, Slieve More, on Achill Island. The rolling green farmland of southern Mayo gives way to harsher landscapes in the north of the county.

Most Irish people are Roman Catholics, and many come to Croagh Patrick (*Cruach Phádraig*) on pilgrimage. It is said that St Patrick, Ireland's patron saint, fasted on this mountain in AD 441. So many pilgrims came to the town of Knock (*Cnoc Muire*) that an international airport was opened there in 1986.

# Poets and farmers

Sligo (*Sligeach*), in northern Connacht, is a county of bays, woods and limestone ridges such as Ben Bulben. Ireland's most famous poet, W B Yeats (1865-1939), grew up here and is buried at Drumcliff. The small, rounded hills, or drumlins, of County Leitrim (*Liatroim*) descend to the valley of the River Shannon. At 258 kilometres (161 miles), the Shannon (*An tSionainn*) is the longest river not only in Ireland but in any of the British Isles. Connacht's only landlocked county, Roscommon (*Ros Comáin*) borders the Shannon and Lough Ree. Sheep and cattle graze on the gentle, low-lying farmland.

*Peat drying in a stack*

# Oceans and mountains

The southwest of Ireland forms the province of Munster (*Cúige Mumhan*). Its coastline reaches out far into the Atlantic Ocean. Shannon airport was built here in the early days of international air travel, as a terminal for transatlantic 'flying boats'.

Many tourists come to the green pastures and the wild coasts of Munster. It is here that the River Shannon finally completes its long river journey. On the coast, the 10 kilometre (6 mile) length of the Cliffs of Moher towers to a dizzying 198 metres (645 feet). The highest point in all Ireland is Carrauntoohill (*Corrán Tuathail*), in the Macgillicuddy's Reeks. The cross on top of the hill stands 1041 metres (3414 feet) above sea-level.

*An ancient tomb, or dolmen, on The Burren, County Clare*

County Clare (*An Clár*) lies on the north bank of the Shannon estuary. The Burren (*Boirinn*) is an extraordinary limestone plateau where there are underground caves and springs. The great slabs of rock seem to be a harsh environment. Yet about 1100 species of plant grow in the cracks and hollows of the rock. These plants include rare orchids and bright blue gentians.

Healing springs have made the small town of Lisdoonvarna (*Lios Dúin Bhearna*) into a spa. It is also known for its matchmaking sessions, at which unmarried farmers may find a bride, and for its folk music festivals.

*The bridge over the River Lee, Cork City*

# The southwest

The lush fields and green hills of County Limerick (*Luimneach*) are rich in history, with medieval abbeys and castles. The city of Limerick dates back to Viking times. St Mary's Cathedral was founded about 800 years ago and the grey stone walls of King John's Castle stand by Thomond Bridge.

County Kerry (*Ciarraí*) enjoys a mild climate in which palms and other exotic plants grow well. Ireland's most westerly point is the Dingle, which was once the haunt of smugglers. The Iveragh peninsula can be explored by a spectacular scenic route, the 'Ring of Kerry'. Killarney (*Cill Áirne*) is set amongst beautiful lakes. The county town of Tralee (*Trá Lí*) is best known for its August festival.

County Cork (*Corcaigh*) stretches eastwards from the Caha mountains and Bantry Bay. Cork is the Republic's second city, and is linked by ferry with South Wales. Markets, shops, quays and warehouses lie beneath the spires of St Finbarr's protestant Cathedral.

## Kissing the Blarney Stone

Why do visitors to Blarney Castle lean backwards over high walls to kiss a stone? To gain the 'gift of the gab', the ability to speak easily and often. It is said that long ago a lord of the castle, Cormac McCarthy, used this gift of fine words to talk his way out of a quarrel with the English.

# Glass and stone

The other large port on Ireland's southern coast is Waterford (*Port Láirge*), in the county of the same name. This was another Viking settlement, which today is famous for its fine crystal glass. Inland, County Tipperary (*Tiobraid Árann*) stretches northwards to the Shannon. The Rock of Cashel is a limestone peak. It was the centre of power for the Kings of Munster for more than 800 years.

*Cutting Waterford crystal glass*

# To the east

St Kevin's Church , Glendalough

The southeastern quarter of Ireland falls within Leinster (*Cúige Laighean*). This province takes in seaports, holiday resorts and sandy beaches. Inland, there are forested hills, lakes and glens. Coastal counties include Wexford (*Loch Garman*), Wicklow (*Cill Mhantáin*), County Dublin (*Baile Átha Cliath*) and Louth (*Lú*).

The rich farmlands of the Central Lowlands are bordered by the Leinster Ridge. They produce the dairy products which are so important to the Irish economy. Inland counties include Kilkenny (*Cill Chainnigh*), Carlow (*Ceatharlach*), Laois, Offaly (*Uibh Fhailí*), Kildare (*Cill Dara*), Westmeath (*An Iarmhí*) and Longford (*An Longfort*).

Ireland's east coast has always been the most populated region. This area has been fought over for much of Ireland's history. Invaders such as the Vikings, the Normans and the English wanted to colonize its fertile land.

## Along the Irish Sea

Vikings from Denmark founded the town of Wexford about 1000 years ago.

*A passenger ferry at Dún Laoghaire harbour*

At Ferrycarrig, on the River Slaney, the Irish National Heritage Centre gives visitors a fascinating look at Irish history. To the southeast of Wexford is Rosslare (*Ros Láir*) Harbour, which is the terminal for sea ferries to Mid-Wales.

In County Wicklow there are beautiful mountains, woods and lakes. Glendalough is an ancient religious site. It was founded more than 1400 years ago by St Kevin, who was a member of the Leinster royal family. The tall round tower of Glendalough was used as a refuge from attacks by Vikings.

There is a grand coastal drive from the seaside town of Bray (*Bré*) northwards to the busy port of Dún Laoghaire. This is the terminal of a ferry service with North Wales. It is the first sight of Ireland for many Dublin-bound visitors.

To the north of Dublin, in County Meath, there are many reminders of Ireland's distant past. The valley of the River Boyne (*An Bhóinn*) has some fascinating Stone Age burial sites. The Hill of Tara was one of the most important sites in the ancient Celtic world. It was here that Ireland's High Kings were crowned.

## Cows and buttercups

Many of the towns in the Central Lowlands have grown from forts which were built during the English occupation of Ireland. Today the meadows are peaceful with browsing cattle. There are bogs and lakes which are full of all kinds of waterfowl. Athlone (*Baile Átha Luain*), on the River Shannon, is a growing market town right at the centre of Ireland. Above its skyline rises the domed Church of Saints Peter and Paul.

### Horse crazy!

The breeding, buying and selling of horses is a national pastime in Ireland, from local horse fairs to world-famous thoroughbred studs. County Kildare is the site of a wide expanse of green turf called the Curragh (*An Currach*). The Irish Derby takes place here each summer. The Curragh is also a breeding place for champion racehorses.

*A race at the Curragh, County Kildare*

# Dublin

The capital city of the Irish Republic is Dublin (*Baile Átha Cliath*). It is built on the banks of the River Liffey (*An Life*), which flows into Dublin Bay beneath the Howth peninsula. The Dublin area is home to nearly a million people. Dublin is a centre of government, law and learning. It is the chief industrial and commercial town in the Republic.

The city is at the heart of a network of communications. There is an international airport, the home base of Ireland's national airline, Aer Lingus. Cross-channel ferries connect Dublin with North Wales, England and the Isle of Man. Railway termini link the capital with other towns and cities. For getting around the Dublin area there is a useful light railway called the DART.

Unlike many other national capitals, Dublin is a friendly city. Office and shop workers, market traders and tourists rub shoulders in bustling streets and city parks. There are famous coffee- and tea-rooms and more than 1000 pubs!

Dublin was founded by Danish Vikings about 1000 years ago. Many of its most elegant buildings and bridges are about 200 years old. Some fine buildings were destroyed during developments in the 1960s and 70s. At that time, high-rise flats were first built in the city. Dublin is now ringed by sprawling suburbs and large housing estates.

*The Halfpenny Bridge over the River Liffey, Dublin*

*Trinity College Library*

## Sights to see

**Trinity College** – Founded in 1592, the university houses the 1200 year-old manuscript of the Book of Kells, a masterpiece of Celtic art. The fine Old Library dates back to 1712. In the summer there is an audio-visual show about the city's history, the Dublin Experience.

**Phoenix Park** – The largest city park in Europe contains the official home of the Irish presidents. A section of the park is taken up by the **Zoological Gardens**.

**National Museum** – This houses priceless treasures such as the Tara brooch and the Ardagh chalice, which are about 1200 years old.

**National Gallery** – This has a fine collection of famous European paintings as well as work by Ireland's greatest artists.

**Irish Life Viking Adventure** – An exciting recreation of the city's first settlement.

# Beside the Liffey

The River Liffey flows through the heart of Dublin. It is bordered by streets called the Quays and by imposing buildings such as the Custom House and the Four Courts. The famous O'Connell Bridge crosses the Liffey near the department stores of O'Connell Street and the large General Post Office. This area was the scene of the 1916 uprising against British rule.

To the south are the fine buildings of Trinity College. Grafton Street is a pedestrian area busy with shoppers and buskers. It leads to the leafy walks and ponds of St Stephen's Green.

Christ Church Cathedral was founded by Dublin's Vikings in AD 1038. St Patrick's Cathedral was built in 1191 on a much older religious site. It is the burial place of Jonathan Swift (1667-1745), who was Dean of the cathedral, and the author of *Gulliver's Travels*.

*The statue of Molly Malone*

# North to Ulster

Three of Ulster's counties form part of the Irish Republic. County Donegal (*Dún na nGall*) stretches northwards from Donegal Bay and the Blue Stack mountains to Lough Swilly and the Inishowen peninsula. Malin Head is the most northerly point of Ireland. This is a land of brooding hills, sparkling sea lochs and small cottages. The gardens and wild glens of Glenveagh National Park lie to the northeast of the Derryveagh range. Donegal is a stronghold of the Irish language and is famous for its tweed.

County Cavan (*Cabhán*) is a hilly land with small loughs which are ideal for fishing and boating holidays. Cavan is said to have one lake for every day of the year! Mount Cuilcagh, in the wild northwest, is the source of the River Shannon.

County Monaghan (*Muineachán*) is a region of small hills, or drumlins, and pasture land. There are old mansions and small market towns. Carrickmacross is well known for its lacemaking.

## Northern Ireland

The Six Counties which make up the rest of Ulster are known for the violence of their recent history. The conflict dates back to the 1600s. At that time, parts of Ireland were forcibly settled by Protestant English and Scots.

Less well known, however, is the peace and natural beauty of the northern countryside. Derry (*Doire*) is a hilly county through which runs the River

*Lough Neagh, Northern Ireland*

Foyle. The county town of Derry, or 'Londonderry', is Northern Ireland's second largest city.

County Tyrone (*Tír Eoghain*) lies to the south across the Sperrin mountains, where small amounts of gold can be mined. Lough Erne divides the beautiful county of Fermanagh (*Fear Manach*).

To the east, Lough Neagh is the largest lake in the British Isles. It is nearly 400 sq. km (250 sq. miles) in area. Armagh (*Ard Mhacha*) is the religious centre for all Ireland. Its county town of the same name has both a Protestant and a Roman Catholic cathedral.

The eastern counties of Antrim (*Aontroim*) and Down (*An Dún*) include the mountains of Antrim and Mourne. This coast has some spectacular features, such as the rocky columns of the Giant's Causeway. St Patrick landed at Strangford Lough in about AD 432. His burial place is at Downpatrick.

Belfast (*Béal Feirste*) is the capital of Northern Ireland. It stands on the River Lagan at the head of Belfast Lough. Belfast has a population of more than 320 000 and is the most industrialized city in Ireland.

*Killard Nature Reserve, County Down*

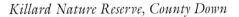

*A view of Belfast city centre from the Lagan Weir*

Queen's University is a famous centre of learning in Belfast. The city has an airport, and ferries sail to England, the Isle of Man and Scotland.

## The search for peace

When Ireland broke away from British rule in 1922, six counties of Ulster remained a part of the United Kingdom. The majority of northerners were Protestants, and most of them supported this union. However, a minority, mostly Roman Catholics, wanted to be part of the Irish Republic. In the 1960s they demanded full civil rights and British troops were sent in amidst growing violence. Self-government in Northern Ireland was replaced with direct rule from London. A number of violent paramilitary groups such as the 'nationalist' Provisional IRA (Irish Republican Army) and the 'loyalist' UVF (Ulster Volunteer Force) led campaigns of terror and bombing in Ireland and England. In 1994 a general ceasefire was declared and peace talks were held with the British government.

# Working and living

The Republic of Ireland is one of the poorer areas of northwestern Europe. However, it has benefitted from membership of the European Union (EU), which it joined in 1973. Farm produce is still a very important part of the economy, but agriculture employs far fewer people than it did 50 years ago. More than a quarter of the labour force work in factories, but nearly half now work in service industries such as tourism. Many people are unemployed. They have to leave Ireland to find work abroad, especially in Britain.

Northern Ireland also has rich farmland, but more of its people are industrial workers than in the south. The EU is funding new business ventures in the north in order to help the peace process.

Ireland has some oil and gas and minerals such as lead and zinc, but on the whole its natural resources are scarce. It does have large amounts of peat. Peat is exported for sale in garden centres and is also a source of power. Twelve per cent of electricity in the Republic is produced by peat-fired power stations. There is now a risk of environmental damage as large areas of valuable wetland are stripped of peat.

Irish farms produce beef, butter, cheese, potatoes, sugar beet and cereal crops. Fish farming and forestry are

*Harvesting corn in Northern Ireland*

*Peat wagons at Shannon power station*

growing in importance. Major Irish industries include brewing and whiskey distillery, textiles, chemicals, computer assembly and tourism.

Northern Ireland is only a short sea voyage from the coalfields of Scotland. Belfast became a centre of heavy industry, including shipbuilding and aircraft manufacture.

## Irish homes

Housing in Ireland comes in all shapes and sizes. In the countryside there are many large, rambling mansions and fine old castles. In the towns there are streets of small, terraced brick houses. They were built for workers about 100 years ago. The high-rise blocks of flats were built in the 1960s. Ireland is famous for its Georgian townhouses, with their elegant porches and windows.

On the west coast the traditional dwellings are smallholdings, or crofts. They are built of stone with thatched roofs. Many of these crofts are now ruined. They have been replaced by trim, brightly painted bungalows. On the edge

of some towns there are sites for caravans and mobile homes. The Irish travelling people live here. They trade in horses, repair tools or work as casual labourers.

## Education and health

Throughout Ireland there is free education. There are various types of schools and colleges, state-owned or private.

In the Republic, many schools are run by religious orders. This is a strongly Roman Catholic country. The Church has traditionally played an important part in education, politics and all aspects of everyday life. Its influence is less, though, than it was 30 years ago.

In Northern Ireland health care is organized in the same way as in Great Britain. There is a free health service, funded by taxation, and private hospitals for those who wish to pay. Most people in the Republic receive free health care. However, people on higher incomes have to pay for some of their treatment.

*A cottage in the west of Ireland*

# Food and drink

Eating at home, each day may start with a large, traditional breakfast of fried eggs, bacon, sausages, toast and strong tea. Lunch, between noon and 2pm, is often the main meal of the day, with meat and vegetables. Supper, between 6 and 8pm, may include tea and cakes or meat or fish.

Diet and eating habits depend on wealth, and as in other parts of Europe, lighter, healthier meals are coming into favour. Today there is more choice of international foods than ever before. Dublin's famous tea and coffee houses are places to spend a morning over the newspapers or to meet up with friends. As in most modern cities, there is no shortage of 'fast food' restaurants and take-aways.

Ireland has many excellent restaurants. Some of these are in beautiful old country houses. Traditional Irish foods include farmhouse fare such as potatoes, cabbage and bacon, as well as shellfish, salmon and trout.

*A variety of fresh shellfish*

*Bewley's oriental café, Dublin*

## Irish favourites

Shellfish dishes include mussels, the famous Clarinbridge oysters, huge lobsters and Dublin Bay prawns. (These are known elsewhere in Europe as Norway lobsters or scampi). Anglers catch brown trout and salmon, which may be gently poached or preserved by smoking. Seaweeds are eaten too, such as dulse or *duileasc*. 'Carrigean moss' is a seaweed which is used like gelatine in milk puddings.

Irish stew is the best known Irish dish. It is made up of mutton, onions, leeks and carrots. Other traditional servings include 'colcannon' (boiled cabbage and potato pie), 'champ' or 'stelk' (onions with cabbage), 'crubeens' (pig knuckle), 'coddle' (bacon, sausage and potato stew) and beef with carrots.

Home baking may produce a yeast-free 'soda bread', or 'tea brack', a delicious currant loaf.

## Stout and strong whiskey

Ireland is world-famous for its alcoholic drinks. Its beers include 'stouts', which are dark and creamy. There is Beamish, Murphy's and the most famous of all, Guinness. This has been brewed in Dublin, beside the River Liffey, since 1759. Whiskey (spelt with an 'e' in Ireland, but not in Scotland) takes its name from the old Gaelic words for 'water of life'. Some people drink whiskey 'neat', that is, without any water. Others add a little water to their whiskey. Many people enjoy 'Irish coffee', which is coffee with cream and whiskey.

### *Sláinte*! 'Your good health!'

The public house or bar is at the centre of Irish life. It is a place where people meet friends, have a drink, tell stories and sing. They play traditional Irish music or listen to a band or a country-singer. Often brightly painted on the outside, the pub may be old-fashioned and unspoiled inside. Some country pubs also serve as shops or village stores.

*Drinks and music in an Irish pub*

# Sports and leisure

Traditional Irish sports are encouraged by the Gaelic Athletic Association, which was founded at Thurles in 1884. These sports are hugely popular. Hurling (*iománaíocht* in Irish) is a very fast game in which a broad, curved stick is used to hit a small, hard leather ball called a *sliotar*.

There are 15 men in a team. The national stadium is Dublin's Croke Park. The most regular all-Ireland champions have been the team from Cork. The cup final, held each September, attracts big crowds. Women play a type of hurling called *camogie*.

*A hurling match between teams from Tipperary and Clare*

*A football match between Northern Ireland and the Republic of Ireland*

Gaelic football is rather like a cross between soccer, rugby, Australian rules football and basketball! The players may catch, kick and punch the round ball, but they must not throw it or carry it for more than four steps. The goal has high posts and a net. The players kick the ball into the net for three points or over the crossbar for one. There are 15 players in each team. The best players may play in the county teams. The Kerry team has won most all-Ireland finals. There are also some women's teams.

## A sporting nation

As in most European countries, soccer is the most popular sport. There are two international sides, Northern Ireland and the Republic of Ireland. Many Irish footballers also play for clubs in Great Britain. During successes in the 1994 World Cup, the Republic's football team became national heroes.

Rugby also has a large following. It is played amongst the four provinces, with one national team representing all Ireland. Rugby fans from all over the world flock to Dublin's Lansdowne Road stadium for international matches.

Irish sporting stars have also made a name for themselves in athletics, cycling and boxing.

The Irish love the outdoor life. Fly-fishing for trout and salmon is one way of enjoying the peaceful countryside. Long hours may be spent standing wader-deep in rivers, casting for trout or salmon. It is a skill that takes many years to perfect.

A day at the races is altogether more noisy and exciting. Racing attracts horse-lovers, gamblers, high society, rogues and millionaires. Best known are the Galway Races, held at Ballybrit each July. The Laytown races are held on a long, sandy beach!

*Flyfishing in Ireland*

# Music and the arts

Traditional Irish music has been made popular around the world by groups such as the Chieftains. It can include wild dance tunes such as jigs, as well as sad, slow airs and unaccompanied singing in Irish Gaelic, or *sean-nós*. Popular instruments are fiddles, accordions, the hand drum or *bodhrán*, the Irish harp, tin whistles, flutes and a type of bagpipe called the Uilleann pipes. An Irish music festival is called a *fleadh*, or *fleá*.

Irish dancing is popular even with very young boys and girls. It requires fast stepping with the feet while the arms are held close to the body.

Irish folk and rock musicians have also made their mark on the world. They include Christy Moore, Van Morrison, U2, Enya and Sinead O'Connor.

All kinds of music are popular locally, including ballads and country music.

## Poets and playwrights

Ireland has a rich tradition of writing and performing, both in the Irish and the English languages.

Some of the heroic tales which the ancient Irish bards recited were written down in the Middle Ages. The 1200 year-old tale, *Táin Bó Cuailnge*, tells the story of how the warriors of Connacht and their allies invaded Ulster on a wild cattle raid. Writing in Irish Gaelic survived English invasions and settlement. In the 1700s, poets such as Aogán O Rathaille, Eoghan Rua O Súilleabháin and Brian Merriman were writing. The translated works of modern poets writing in Irish, such as Nuala Ní Dhomhnaill (b.1952), have reached a world audience.

*Playing accordions and tin whistles*

*A painting of W B Yeats, by Augustus John*

Irish writing in the English language began in the 1700s. Writers such as Oscar Wilde (1854-1900), George Bernard Shaw (1856-1950) and W B Yeats (1865-1939) are world-famous.

John M Synge (1871-1909) and Sean O'Casey (1884-1964) also had plays performed at Dublin's Abbey Theatre. This theatre opened in 1904 and became the centre of many a political and artistic storm. The work of novelist James Joyce (1882-1941) and his friend the playwright Samuel Beckett (1906-89), shocked and puzzled some readers, but inspired many more. Modern writers include the poets Seamus Heaney and Nuala Ní Dhomhnaill, and the novelists Jennifer Johnston and Roddy Doyle.

# Art and design

The ancient Celts produced wonderful designs of interlaced knots and animals and birds. When Christianity came to Ireland more than 1500 years ago, these designs were taken up by metalworkers, stonemasons and the monks who copied out holy scriptures. Masterpieces of this period include the Book of Durrow (AD 675) and the Book of Kells (AD 804).

In our own century, the best known Irish painter was probably Jack B Yeats (1871-1957), the brother of the poet. He is remembered for his scenes of Irish life and his pictures of fairs and circuses.

*A page from the Book of Kells*

# Gaels and Vikings

We know that Stone Age hunters were living in Ireland in about 7000 BC. There are many stone burial chambers dating from about 3500 BC. No less than 40 of these sites survive today in the Brugh na Bóinne region between Slane and Tullyallen. The tomb at Newgrange is one of the most extraordinary sites in Europe. The stones there are carved with strange zig-zag, wave and spiral patterns.

In later ages legends and superstitions grew up around eerie sites like these. Farmers and villagers thought they must be the homes of 'little people' or fairies, who would steal children or put people to sleep for hundreds of years!

High on the cliffs of County Mayo, at a site called Céide Fields, a vast network of Stone Age Fields is being dug from the bog. Archaeologists are piecing together a picture of Stone Age Ireland.

Between 1750 and 500 BC the secrets of metal-working in copper, bronze, gold and iron began to reach Ireland. They were brought by waves of new settlers from the south and east.

The Celtic way of life was spreading through northern Europe at this period. The Celtic languages and cultures grew up in central and western Europe. They spread westwards to Spain and eastwards as far as Turkey. The British Isles were the centres of two main Celtic groups. The Britons of Great Britain were the ancestors of today's Welsh, Cornish and Breton people. The Gaels of Ireland were the ancestors of the Irish, Scots Gaelic and Manx people.

*A Stone Age site, Cushendall, County Antrim*

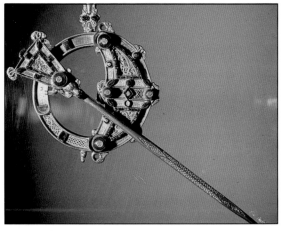

*The Tara Brooch, made in the 8th century*

The Gaels were the only group of Celts to escape conquest by the growing power of Rome. This was the age of chariots and strongholds, of cattle raids and tribal wars. There were many local kings and queens, but above them all were the High Kings, who held court at Tara. From about AD 300, a form of writing called 'ogham' was developed. It was made up of criss-cross lines, carved on the edges of stones.

As Roman power collapsed on the other side of the Irish Sea, Irish raiders (called 'Scots') began to raid and settle much of northwestern Great Britain. This area later became known as Scotland.

### Heroic deeds

The tales of the ancient Celts still inspire us today. They tell of bravery, trickery and magic. Legendary characters included Queen Maeve of Connacht, Finn MacCool and Cuchulainn, the wiliest warrior of all.

In about AD 432, St Patrick, a British Celt, came to preach Christianity to the Irish people. A Celtic Church grew up, which made the lands around the Irish Sea into a centre of civilization. Most of the rest of Europe was being torn apart by disastrous wars. Monasteries were founded here and great works of art were inspired by the new faith.

## The coming of the longships

The churches and monasteries of Ireland offered rich pickings for Viking raiders from Denmark and Norway. Between AD 795 and 1000 their warships sailed into river estuaries and sea loughs. They looted, burned and then stayed to build settlements such as Dublin and Wexford.

Sometimes there were alliances between the Vikings and the Gaels, but at Clontarf in 1014 the Irish united under their High King. He was a great soldier called Brian Boru (or *Bóroimhe*). He was killed in the battle, but the Dublin Vikings were defeated at last.

*The Ardagh Chalice, made around AD 720*

# Rule from England

In 1066 England was conquered by Normans, who were the descendants of Viking settlers in northern France. The Norman lords soon began to seize land in Wales and Scotland. In 1168 the King of Leinster, Dermot MacMurrough, called in these Normans as his allies in a war with other Irish kings.

Before long, Norman warlords such as 'Strongbow' (Richard Fitzgilbert de Clare) were taking large areas of Irish territory as their own. The Pope in Rome, who was the most powerful person in Europe during the Middle Ages, now declared that King Henry II of England, was overlord of all Ireland.

However, the Normans soon began to adopt the Irish way of life and language. By the end of the Middle Ages, the English kings controlled only a small area around Dublin, known as 'the Pale'. Beyond the Pale, the Irish way of life continued.

In the 1500s England broke away from the Roman Catholic Church. It became a Protestant country. English kings and queens, eager to gain new territory, launched a series of savage wars against the Catholic Irish. Even during the period when the English had no kings, they continued the attack. After an Irish rebellion at Drogheda in 1649, the English leader, or 'Lord Protector', Oliver Cromwell, massacred the whole population of the town. The land of Irish Catholics was seized and given to Protestant settlers from England and Scotland.

*An Irish chief's last fight, from a book made in 1581*

*William of Orange at the Battle of the Boyne*

# Rebellion and famine

In 1685 a Roman Catholic came to the throne of both England and Scotland. James (II of England, VII of Scotland), soon lost his throne to a Dutch Protestant, William of Orange. The Irish rose up in support of James, but he was finally defeated by William at the Battle of the Boyne, in 1690. 'King Billy's' victory is still celebrated by Unionists in Northern Ireland.

In 1782 Ireland was granted its own parliament, but this was ended after a nationalist rebellion in 1798. The United Irishmen (both Protestant *and* Catholic) revolted under the leadership of Theobald Wolfe Tone. They were supported by revolutionary troops from France, but were brutally defeated. The Irish parliament was abolished and in 1800 Ireland became part of the United Kingdom. Irish Catholics were refused the vote until 1829. Their leader was the great campaigner Daniel O'Connell, the 'Liberator'. Nationalist groups such as the Young Ireland Party were formed.

In 1845-46 the potato harvest failed because of a plant disease called blight. Ireland depended on the potato crop for its food, and it is thought that about a million people died of hunger during the terrible famine that followed.

For most Irish people, the nineteenth century was a grim period. English landowners grew rich from estates they did not visit. Many tenants fought this injustice by refusing to pay their rents. Many poor peasants were thrown out of their houses and made homeless.

Several nationalist groups were formed. The Irish Republican Brotherhood (whose members were called 'Fenians' after the legendary warriors of Finn MacCool) was founded in 1858. In the 1870s Charles Stewart Parnell, of the Home Rule League, tried to obtain self-rule through the British parliament.

*Tenants evicted, their homes burned, 1887*

# Free Ireland

The United Kingdom finally agreed to grant Home Rule to Ireland in 1914. The Ulster Protestants, under Edward Carson, refused to accept Home Rule, and armed themselves for a civil war. However, it was in that year that the First World War broke out. Home Rule was suspended and many young Irishmen joined the British army.

In 1916, at Easter, there was an armed rising in Dublin. A small rebel force, made up of the Irish Volunteers and the Irish Citizen Army, was led by Patrick Pearse and James Connolly. They held out for four days in Dublin's General Post Office, but were shelled into defeat by the British army. At first this Easter Rising received little widespread support. However, after the British executed 17 leading republicans by firing squad and made many arrests, public opinion in Ireland changed.

In 1918 the First World War ended. At the general election Ireland voted in a nationalist political party called *Sinn Féin* ('We ourselves'). The Irish Republican Army (IRA) led uprisings in many parts of Ireland, so in 1920 the British sent in special army units. There were many terrible acts of violence.

## From Free State to Republic

In 1922 the British government agreed to the creation of an Irish Free State. Ireland, apart from six counties of Ulster, was to be given limited independence.

*The Easter Rising, Dublin, 1916*

Some nationalists, such as Michael Collins, felt this was the best deal they could achieve. Éamon de Valera and the IRA still demanded an independent republic including the six counties. A bitter war broke out between the two groups and Michael Collins was assassinated.

In 1927 Éamon de Valera became president, and began to untie the remaining links with Britain. In 1937 the Irish Free State changed its name to *Éire*. It remained neutral in the Second World War (1939-45) and finally became the Republic of Ireland in 1949. It remained divided but at peace until the late 1960s.

## New troubles

In the north, Roman Catholics complained that they were not being treated fairly. In 1969 they organized marches to protest. Violence broke out and British troops were sent in. The IRA renewed its fight, but declared a ceasefire in 1972. Its place was taken by violent new paramilitary groups. These included the Provisional IRA and the Irish National Liberation Army (INLA).

*An army patrol in Newry, 1987*

'Loyalist' groups who supported the union with Britain included the Ulster Volunteer Force (UVF) and the Ulster Freedom Fighters (UFF). Campaigns of murder and terror soon spread beyond Northern Ireland to the Republic and to England. The violence stopped in 1994, when the paramilitary groups declared a ceasefire. This was broken early in 1996 and permanent peace seems doubtful.

### Ireland's future

Peace in the north remains the most important political issue for all Irish people, but it is not the only one. Young people in Ireland today might discuss the role of religion in modern Ireland; the EU and the economy; pollution in the Irish Sea; emigration; the state of the Irish language, and Ireland's role abroad. Many Irish troops wear the blue beret of the United Nations forces, and many young Irish people work for aid agencies overseas.

*Children in the Mourne Mountains*

# Fact file

## Government

In the Republic, the head of state is the President or *Uachtarán*. The Prime Minister or *Taoiseach* is the head of the government. The Parliament is made up of two houses. The House of Representatives (*Dáil*) has 166 elected Members of Parliament, while the Senate has 60 nominated members. The three biggest political parties are *Fianna Fáil*, *Fine Gael* and Labour.

Northern Ireland sends elected Members of Parliament to the British House of Commons. The main political parties include the Official Unionists, the Democratic Unionists, the Social Democratic and Labour Party (SDLP) and *Sinn Féin*. The UK government manages Northern Ireland's affairs through a Northern Ireland Office.

## Flags

The flag of the Republic dates back to 1848. It is a tricolour of green (from the original flag of a free Ireland), white (for peace) and orange (the colour of William of Orange, to show unity with the protestants). Flags of Northern Ireland include the Union Flag of the United Kingdom and the Red Hand of Ulster.

## National anthems

The anthem of the Republic is *Amhrán na bhFiann* ('Song of the Soldiers'). The anthem of Northern Ireland is 'God Save the Queen'.

## Money

The currency of the Republic is the *Punt* or Irish pound (£) which is divided into 100 *pingin* or pence. The Northern Ireland currency is the pound sterling (£), which also equals 100 pence.

## Religion

Roman Catholics form 94 per cent of the population in the Republic and 28 per cent in Northern Ireland. Protestant churches include the Anglican Church of Ireland, the Irish Presbyterian, the Free Presbyterian and the Methodist Churches.

## Public holidays

Special holidays in Ireland include the Protestant Orangemen's Day in the north (12 July), and St Patrick's Day (17 March), the national day of the Republic. St Patrick's Day is celebrated by people of Irish descent all over the world.

## News and broadcasting

The best known newspapers include the *Irish Times*, the *Cork Examiner* and the *Belfast Telegraph*. There are also special Irish editions of the United Kingdom newspapers. There are two main Irish-language newspapers, *Lá* (a Belfast daily) and *Anois* (a Sunday paper in *Éire*).

Ireland receives two Republic-based television channels, Network 2 and RTE 1. BBC Ulster broadcasts in the north and UK television channels are also received.

## Some famous people

**St Patrick** (cAD385-461), Ireland's patron saint, introduced Christianity

**St Brigid** (453-523) was a nun. She is Ireland's patroness saint

**St Brendan** (484-577) was an explorer who sailed the Atlantic Ocean

**St Columba** (521-97) was a monk and missionary

**Brian Boru** (926-1014) was the king who finally defeated the Vikings

**Grace O'Malley** (Gráinne Ni Mháille, b1530), was a woman pirate chief

**Theobald Wolfe Tone** (1763-98) led an armed uprising with French help

**Daniel O'Connel**l (1775-1847) was a lawyer and political campaigner

**Lady Isabella Gregory** (1852-1932) wrote plays and founded the Abbey Theatre in Dublin in 1904

**Edward Carson** (1854-1935) was a violent opponent of Home Rule

**Constance Markiewicz** (1868-1927) was a nationalist and rebel

**Éamon de Valera** (1882-1975) led the Easter Rising in Dublin in 1916 and became Ireland's first president

**Ian Paisley** (1926- ) is a N Ireland minister and Democratic Unionist MP

**Mary Peters** (1939- ), N Ireland athlete and Olympic gold medal winner

**Mary Robinson** (1944- ) is the first female president of the Republic

**Gerry Adams** (1948- ) is the *Sinn Féin* leader who agreed to the 1994 ceasefire

**Barry McGuigan** (1951- ) became a world boxing champion

**Bob Geldof** (1954- ) is a pop star who organised famine relief for Africa

## Some key events in history

**3000 BC**: Stone Age burial chambers

**1750 BC**: Irish Bronze Age

**500 BC**: Celtic Iron Age in Ireland

**AD 432**: St Patrick arrives in Ireland

**795**: First Viking raid on Ireland

**1014**: Vikings defeated by Brian Boru at the Battle of Clontarf

**1169**: Normans arrive from England

**1175**: Henry II of England claims to be overlord of Ireland

**1556**: The start of enforced Protestant settlement ('plantation')

**1594**: Start of nine years of war in Ulster, attempt to expel English

**1649**: Cromwell sacks Ireland

**1690**: The Battle of the Boyne

**1795**: The Orange Order founded

**1798**: Defeat of United Irishmen and their French allies

**1800**: Union with United Kingdom

**1842**: Young Ireland founded

**1845**: Failure of potato crop and famine

**1858**: Founding of the Irish Republican Brotherhood (the 'Fenians')

**1884**: Founding of the Gaelic Athletic Association

**1916**: The Easter Rising in Dublin

**1922**: The Irish Free State is founded, civil war

**1937**: The Free State becomes known as *Éire*

**1949**: Ireland becomes a full republic

**1969**: Civil rights marches and start of new troubles in Northern Ireland

**1973**: Both the Republic and Northern Ireland join the EEC (today's EU)

**1994**: Ceasefire and peace talks in Northern Ireland

# Index

9611 040
LEAA